A LETTER TO THE READER

Hello, my dear reader! I am so grateful that you have chosen to read this book! It is inspired by *The Little Flowers of Saint Francis*, translated by W. Heywood, which changed my life.

All the money I make from this book will go to charities that promote spiritual awareness and growth.

I suggest that you read one or two stories every day, taking time to soak in each one.

I pray that the little flowers here will bring great joy to your heart and God's light into your life!

TABLE OF CONTENTS

A NOTE ON SOURCES

When not out of public domain, sources are listed in the footnotes. Minor edits have been made to the texts to preserve clarity

PRAYER OF SAINT THERESA

Let nothing disturb you,

Let nothing frighten you,

All things are passing away:

God never changes.

Patience obtains all things.

Whoever has God lacks nothing;

God alone suffices.

MANY NAMES OF ONE GOD[1]

"You may say that there are many errors and superstitions in another religion. I should reply: Suppose there are. Every religion has errors. Everyone thinks that his watch alone gives the correct time. It is enough to have yearning for God. It is enough to love Him and feel attracted to Him: Don't you know that God is the Inner Guide? He sees the longing of our heart and the yearning of our soul. Suppose a man has several sons. The older boys address him distinctly as 'Baba' or 'Papa', but the babies can at best call him 'Ba' or 'Pa'. Now, will the father be angry with those who address him in this indistinct way? The father knows that they too are calling him, only they cannot pronounce his name well. All children are the same to the father.

[1] From the Gospel of Ramakrishna

Likewise, the devotees call on God alone, though by different names. They call on one Person only. God is one, but His names are many."

SOUL FOOD[2]

Everybody on earth knowing

That beauty is beautiful

Makes ugliness

Everybody knowing

That goodness is good

Makes wickedness

For being and nonbeing

Arise together;

Hard and easy

Complete each other;

---

[2] From the *Tao Te Ching* translated by Ursula LeGuin

Long and short

Shape each other;

High and low

Depend on each other;

Note and voice

Make the music together;

Before and after

Follow each other.

That's why the wise soul

Does without doing,

Teaches without talking

The things of this world

Exist, they are;

You can't refuse them.

To bear and not to own;

To act and not lay claim;

To do the work and let it go:

For just letting it go

Is what makes it stay.

LIKE A SILKWORM WEAVING[3]

Like a silkworm weaving

her house with love

from her marrow

and dying

in her body's threads

winding tight, round

and round,

I burn

desiring what the heart desires.

Cut through, O lord,

my heart's greed,

and show me

---

[3] This poem by Mahadeviyakka was translated by AK Ramanujan

your way out,

O lord as white as jasmine

LETTER BY FRANK LAUBACH[4]

Knowing God better and better is an achievement of friendship. "When two persons fall in love there may be such a strong feeling of fellowship, such a delight in the friend's presence, that one may lose oneself in the deepening discovery of another person. The self and the person loved become equally real.

There are, therefore, three questions which we may ask: "Do you believe in God?" That is not getting very far. "The devils believe and tremble." Second, "Are you acquainted with God?" We are acquainted with people with whom we have had some business dealings. Third,

---

[4] From *Letters by a Modern Mystic* by Frank C. Laubach.

“Is God your friend?” or putting this another way, “Do you love God?”

It is this third stage that is really vital. How is it to be achieved? Precisely as any friendship is achieved – by doing things together. The depth and intensity of the friendship will depend upon the variety and extent of the things we do and enjoy together. Will the friendship be constant? That again depends upon the permanence of our common interests and upon whether or not our interests grow into ever-widening circles, so that we do not stagnate. The highest friendship demands growth. “It must be progressive as life itself is progressive.” Friends must walk together; they cannot long stand still together, for that means death to friendship and to life.

Friendship with God is the friendship of child with parent. As an ideal son grows daily into closer relationship with his father, so we may grow into closer love with God by widening into His interests and thinking His thoughts and sharing His enterprises.

Far more than any other device of God to create love was the cross where the *lovingest* person the world has known hangs loving through all His pain. That cross has become the symbol of religion and of love for a third of the world because it touches the deepest depths of human love.

All I have said is mere words, until one sets out helping God right wrongs, helping God help the helpless, loving and talking it over with God. Then there comes a great sense of the close-up, warm intimate heart of reality. God simply creeps in and you *know* He is here in your heart. He has become your friend by working along with you.

So, if anybody were to ask me how to find God I should say at once, hunt out the deepest need you can find and forget all about your own comfort while you try to meet that need. Talk to God about it, and — He will be there. You will know it.

THE VISION OF FRIAR JOHN OF ALVERNIA[5]

The aforesaid Friar John of Alvernia, in that he had perfectly suffocated every worldly and temporal delight and consolation, and had set all his joy and all his hope in God, was given marvelous consolations and revelations by the Divine Goodness, and especially on the festivals of Christ; wherefore, on a time when the Festival of the Nativity of Christ drew nigh, whereon he looked with confidence to receive from God consolation of the sweet humanity of Jesus, the Holy Ghost put in his heart such great and exceeding love and fervor for the charity of Christ, whereby He humbled Himself to take upon Him our humanity, that of a verity it seemed

[5] From *Little Flowers of Saint Francis*, translated by W. Heywood

to him that his soul was drawn forth from his body and that it burned like a furnace. Whereupon not being able to endure such ardors, he was in agony and altogether melting away, and cried out with a loud voice; because, through the violent impulse of the Holy Ghost and through the too great fervor of love, he could not restrain himself from crying out. And in that hour wherein this measureless fervor came upon him, there came therewith so sure and certain a hope of salvation that, for nothing in the world, could he believe that, if he were then to die, he must pass through the pains of purgatory; and this love endured with him for six full months, albeit he felt not that excessive fervor continually, but it came upon him at certain hours of the day. And during this time he received marvelous visitations and consolations from God; and oftentimes he was rapt in ecstasy, even as that friar, who first wrote of these things, saw. Among the which times, he was one night so elevated and rapt in God that he beheld in Him, the Creator, all created things, both celestial and terrestrial, and all their perfections and grades and separate orders. And then he clearly understood how every created thing represented its Creator, and how God is above, and within, and outside, and beside all created things. Thereafter, he discerned one God in Three Persons, and Three Persons in one God, and the infinite charity which caused the Son of God to become incarnate in obedience to the Father. And, finally, he perceived, in that vision, how that there was no other way whereby the soul could go to God and have eternal life, save only through Christ the blessed, who is the Way, the Truth and the Life of the soul.

THE FINAL STATE[6]

The ineffable tale

of that final simple state:

it's utterly different

It can't be weighed on a scale,

can't be whittled down.

It doesn't feel heavy

and doesn't feel light.

It has no rain, no sea,

no sun or shade.

It doesn't contain

creation or destruction.

No life, no death exist in it,

---

[6] This poem by Kabir was translated by Vinay Dhardwaker

no grief, no joy.

Both solitude and blissful union

are absent from it.

It has no up or down, no high or low.

It doesn't contain either night or day.

There's no water, no air,

no fire that flares again and again.

The true master permeates everything there.

The eternal one remains

unmoving, imperceptible, unknowable.

You can attain Him

with the Guru's grace.

Kabir says,

sacrifice yourself to the Guru

and remain ensconced

in the true community.

FROM THE LARGE JUG, DRINK[7]

From the large jug, drink the wine of Unity,

So that from your heart you can wash away the futility of life's grief.

But like this large jug, still keep the heart expansive.

Why would you want to keep the heart captive, like an unopened bottle of wine?

With your mouth full of wine, you are selfless

And will never boast of your own abilities again.

---

[7] This poem by Hafiz was translated by Thomas Rain Crowe

Be like the humble stone at your feet rather than striving to be like a sublime cloud:

the more you mix colors of deceit, the more colorless your ragged wet coat will get.

Connect the heart to the wine, so that it has body,

Then cut off the neck of hypocrisy and piety of this new man.

Be like Hafiz: Get up and make an effort. Don't lie around like a bum.

He who throws himself at the Beloved's feet is like a workhorse and will

be rewarded with boundless pastures and eternal rest.

ON SEEING GOD EVERYWHERE[8]

Master[9]: "But this is not possible without intense love of God. One sees nothing but God everywhere when one loves Him with great intensity. It is like a person with jaundice, who sees everything yellow. Then one feels, 'I am verily He'.

"A drunkard, deeply intoxicated, says, 'Verily I am Kali!' The Gopis[10], intoxicated with love, exclaimed, 'Verily I am Krishna!'

"One who thinks of God, day and night, beholds Him everywhere. It is like a man's seeing flames on all sides after he

---

[8] From the Gospel of Sri Ramakrishna

[9] Master refers to Sri Ramakrishna. M. refers to Sri M, the author of the Gospel.

[10] Kali is a form of Durga — a Hindu goddess. The Gopis were cowherds deeply devoted to Krishna

has gazed fixedly at one flame for some time."

"But that isn't the real flame", flashed through M.'s mind.

Sri Ramakrishna, who could read a man's inmost thought, said: "One doesn't lose consciousness by thinking of Him who is all Spirit, all Consciousness. Shivanath once remarked that too much thinking about God confounds the brain. Thereupon I said to him, 'How can one become unconscious by thinking of Consciousness?'"

M: "Yes, sir, I realize that. It isn't like thinking of an unreal object. How can a man lose his intelligence if he always fixes his mind on Him whose very nature is eternal Intelligence?"

Master (*with pleasure*): "It is through God's grace that you understand that.

The doubts of the mind will not disappear without His grace. Doubts do not disappear without Self-realization.

“But one need not fear anything if one has received the grace of God. It is rather easy for a child to stumble if he holds his father's hand; but there can be no such fear if the father holds the child's hand. A man does not have to suffer any more if God, in His grace, removes his doubts and reveals Himself to him. But this grace descends upon him only after he has prayed to God with intense yearning of heart and practiced spiritual discipline. The mother feels compassion for her child when she sees him running about breathlessly. She has been hiding herself; now she appears before the child.”

“But why should God make us run about?” thought M.

Immediately Sri Ramakrishna said: "It is His will that we should run about a little. Then it is great fun. God has created the world in play, as it were. This is called Mahamaya, the Great Illusion. Therefore, one must take refuge in the Divine Mother, the Cosmic Power Itself. It is She who has bound us with the shackles of illusion. The realization of God is possible only when those shackles are severed."

I AM UNMOVABLE!

A monk searching after enlightenment decided that he needed to isolate himself to find true peace. He sailed far away to a tiny, deserted island in the middle of the ocean. He made a vow: he would never be affected by emotion. Neither anger nor sadness would touch him. He would embark on a great quest for joy, and until he found it, he would stay on the island.

One day, he felt a deep, reinvigorating peace. "I am finally enlightened!" he triumphantly declared. He resolved to write a letter to his previous abbot. "I have done it! I have achieved enlightenment. Nothing in this world can touch me. Not even the force of all the eight winds combined can move me. I have realized life's ultimate goal! Thank you so much for your teachings— I couldn't have done it without you!"

He received a response after a few weeks. The monk quickly opened the letter, and to his surprise, he saw that it contained only one word: "Fart!" Angered, the monk sailed back to his abbot. "You will explain this to me!" he yelled. "You must be jealous of my accomplishment!" His teacher calmly responded to him. "You said that all the eight winds combined couldn't move you, yet you were brought all the way across the ocean with just a fart."

A CRYSTAL RIM[11]

The
Earth
Lifts its glass to the sun
And light — light
Is poured.

A bird
Comes and sits on a crystal rim
And from my forest cave I
Hear singing.

So I run to the edge of existence
And join my soul in love.

I lift my heart to God
And grace is poured.

An emerald bird rises from inside me

---

[11] This poem by Hafiz was translated by Daniel Ladinsky

And now sits
Upon the Beloved's
Glass.

I have left that dark cave forever.
My body has blended with His.

I lay my wing
As a bridge to you

So that you can join us
Singing.

THE ELEPHANT AND GOD[12]

Let me tell you a story. In a forest there lived a holy man who had many disciples. One day he taught them to see God in all beings and, knowing this, to bow low before them all. A disciple went to the forest to gather wood for the sacrificial fire. Suddenly he heard an outcry: “Get out of the way! A mad elephant is coming!” All but the disciple of the holy man took to their heels. He reasoned that the elephant was also God in another form. Then why should he run away from it? He stood still, bowed before the animal, and began to sing its praises. The Mahut of the elephant was shouting: 'Run away! Run away!' But the disciple didn't move. The animal seized him with its trunk, cast him to one side, and went on its way.

---

[12] Parable of Sri Ramakrishna

Hurt and bruised, the disciple lay unconscious on the ground. Hearing what had happened, his teacher and his brother disciples came to him and carried him to the hermitage.

With the help of some medicine, he soon regained consciousness. Someone asked him, 'You knew the elephant was coming – why didn't you leave the place?' 'But', he said, 'our teacher has told us that God Himself has taken all these forms, of animals as well as men. Therefore, thinking it was only the elephant God that was coming, I didn't run away.' At this the teacher said: 'Yes, my child, it is true that the elephant God was coming; but the Mahut God forbade you to stay there. Since all are manifestations of God, why didn't you trust the Mahut's words? You should have heeded the words of the Mahut God.' It is said in the scriptures that water is a form of God. But some water is fit to be used for worship, some water for washing the face, and some only for washing plates or dirty linen. This last sort cannot be used for drinking or for a holy purpose. In like manner, God undoubtedly dwells in the hearts of all – holy and unholy, righteous, and unrighteous; but a man should not have dealings with the unholy, the wicked, the impure. He must not be intimate with them. With some of them he may exchange words, but with others he shouldn't even go that far. He should keep aloof from such people.

NOT WANTING[13]

The five colors

Blind our eyes.

The five notes

Deafen our ears.

The five flavors

Dull our taste.

Racing, chasing, and hunting,

Drives our people crazy.

Trying to get rich

Ties people in knots.

---

[13] This is a section from the Tao Te Ching translated by Ursula LeGuin

So the wise soul

Watches with the inner

Not the outward eye,

Letting that go,

Keeping this.

PICK IT UP AND READ[14]

Now when deep reflection had drawn up out of the secret depths of my soul all my misery and had heaped it up before the sight of my heart, there arose a mighty storm, accompanied by a mighty rain of tears. That I might give way fully to my tears and lamentations, I stole away from Alypius[15], for it seemed to me that solitude was more appropriate for the business of weeping. I went far enough away that I could feel that even his presence was no restraint upon me. This was the way I felt at the time, and he realized it. I suppose I had said something before I started up and he noticed that the sound of my voice was choked with weeping. And so he

---

[14] From the Confessions of St. Augustine, translated by Albert C. Outler

[15] Alypius was one of St. Augustine's closest friends

stayed alone, where we had been sitting together, greatly astonished. I flung myself down under a fig tree — how I know not — and gave free course to my tears. The streams of my eyes gushed out an acceptable sacrifice to Thee. And, not indeed in these words, but to this effect, I cried to Thee: "And Thou, O Lord, how long? How long, O Lord? Wilt Thou be angry forever? Oh, remember not against us our former iniquities." For I felt that I was still enthralled by them. I sent up these sorrowful cries: "How long, how long? Tomorrow and tomorrow? Why not now? Why not this very hour make an end to my uncleanness?"

I was saying these things and weeping in the most bitter contrition of my heart, when suddenly I heard the voice of a boy or a girl, I know not which — coming from the neighboring house, chanting over and over again, “Pick it up, read it; pick it up, read it.” Immediately I ceased weeping and began most earnestly to think whether it was usual for children in some kind of game to sing such a song, but I could not remember ever having heard the like. So, damming the torrent of my tears, I got to my feet, for I could not but think that this was a divine command to open the Bible and read the first passage I should light upon. For I had heard how [Saint] Anthony, accidentally coming into church while the gospel was being read, received the admonition as if what was read had been addressed to him: “Go and sell what you have and give it to the poor, and you shall have treasure in heaven; and come and follow me.” By such an oracle he was forthwith converted to Thee. So I quickly returned to the bench where Alypius was sitting, for there I had put down the apostle’s book when I had left there. I snatched it up, opened it, and in silence read the paragraph on which my eyes first fell: "Not in rioting and drunkenness, not in chambering and wantonness, not in strife and envying, but put on the Lord Jesus Christ, and make no provision for the flesh to fulfill the lusts thereof." I wanted to read no further, nor did I need to. For instantly, as the sentence ended, there was infused in my heart something like the light of full certainty and all the gloom of doubt vanished away.

Closing the book, then, and putting my finger or something else for a mark I began — now with a tranquil countenance — to tell it all to Alypius. And he in turn disclosed to me what had been going on in himself, of which I knew nothing. He asked to see what I had read. I showed him, and he looked on even further than I had read. I had not known what followed. But indeed it was this, "Him that is weak in the faith, receive." This he applied to himself, and told me so. By these words of warning he was strengthened, and by exercising his good resolution and purpose — all very much in keeping with his character, in which, in these respects, he was always far different from and better than I — he joined me in full commitment without any restless hesitation.

Then we went in to my mother, and told her what happened, to her great joy. We explained to her how it had occurred — and she leaped for joy triumphant; and she blessed Thee, who art "able to do exceedingly abundantly above all that we ask or think." For she saw that Thou hadst granted her far more than she had ever asked for in all her pitiful and doleful lamentations. For Thou didst so convert me to Thee that I sought neither a wife nor any other of this world's hopes, but set my feet on that rule of faith which so many years before Thou hadst showed her in her dream about me. And so Thou didst turn her grief into gladness more plentiful than she had ventured to desire, and dearer and purer than the desire she used to cherish of having grandchildren of my flesh.

THIS WORLD AS A DREAM[16]

A man lives in a town for many years

But when he sleeps

another town appears before his eyes,

one full of good and bad,

And he forgets the former life he had —

he never forgets

the former life he had —

He never thinks "Surely there's something wrong here,

This isn't my town, and I don't belong here,

I lived once in that other place ... "Instead

[16] A poem by Rumi translated by Dick Davis

He's certain here's where he was born and bred.

So it's not strange then if the soul's unable to

Recall where it once came to be and grew,

Since this world's

like a sleep as deep as night

Or like a cloud that hides the stars from sight.

SAINT FRANCIS EXPLAINS PERFECT JOY[17]

On a cold winter's day, Saint Francis walked with Brother Leo from Perugia to the Porziuncola. Because of their poverty, they suffered much in the cold. At one point, Saint Francis said to Brother Leo: "If God desired that the Friars Minor should serve as a great example of holiness to all people in all lands, please write down that this would not be perfect joy." At some point later in their journey, Saint Francis said to Brother Leo: "If the Friars Minor could make the lame walk; if we could straighten the crooked; if we could chase away demons; if we could give sight to the blind and speech to the dumb; and even if we could raise the

---

[17] From *Little Flowers of Saint Francis* (Assisi Project Version)

dead after four days, please write down and note carefully that this would not be perfect joy."

Soon after, Saint Francis said to Brother Leo: "If the Friars Minor could speak every language; if they knew everything about science; if they could explain all the scriptures; if they could predict the future and reveal the secrets of every soul, please write down and note carefully that this would not be perfect joy." After a few more steps, Saint Francis cried: "Brother Leo, little one of God! If the Friars Minor could sing like angels; if they could explain the movements of the stars; if they knew everything about all animals, birds, fish, plants, stones, trees, and all men, please write down and note carefully that this would not be perfect joy." Finally, Saint Francis cried again: "Brother Leo, if the Friars Minor could preach and thus convert every person to faith in Christ, please write down and note carefully that even this is not perfect joy."

When this manner of discourse lasted for several miles, Brother Leo, who had been thinking about these sayings, asked: "Father Francis, I pray that you will teach me about perfect joy." Saint Francis answered: "If we arrive at the Porziuncola and if we are drenched with rain and trembling with cold, covered in mud and exhausted from hunger; and if we knock on the convent gate; and if we are not recognized by the porter; and if he tells us that we are impostors who seek to deceive the world and steal from the poor; and if he refuses to open the gate; and if he leaves us outside, exposed to the rain and snow, suffering from cold and hunger; then if we embrace the injustice, cruelty, and contempt with patience, without complaining; and if we believe in faith, love, and humility that the porter knew us but was told by God to reject us, then, my dear Brother Leo, please write down and note carefully that this is perfect joy!"

Saint Francis then said: "Brother Leo, if we knock again and if the porter drives us away with curses and blows; and if he accuses us of robbery and other crimes; and if we embrace this with patience without complaining; and if we believe in faith, love, and humility that the porter knew us but was told by God to reject us again, then, my dear Brother Leo, please write down and note carefully that this is perfect joy!" Saint Francis said once more: "If urged by cold and hunger, we knock again; if we call again to the porter; if we plead to him with many tears to open the gate and to give us shelter out of love for God; and if he returns more angry than ever; and if he calls us annoying rascals and beats us with a knotted stick; and if he throws us to the ground, rolls us in the snow, and beats us again with the knotted stick; and if we bear these injuries with patience without complaining; and if we think upon the sufferings of our Blessed Crucified Lord, then, most beloved Brother Leo, please write down and note carefully that this, finally, is perfect joy!"

Finally, Saint Francis said: "Brother Leo, please listen to me. Above all gifts of the Holy Spirit, that Christ Jesus gives to his friends is the grace to overcome oneself, to accept willingly, out of love for Him, all contempt, all discomfort, all injury, and all suffering. In this and all other gifts, we ourselves should not boast because all things are gifts from God. Remember the words of Saint Paul:

‘What do you have that you did not receive from God? And if you did receive it, why do you boast as if it were not a gift (1 Corinthians 4:7)?’ But in the cross of afflictions and suffering, we truly can see glory because as Saint Paul says again: ‘May I never boast of anything except the cross of our Lord Jesus Christ, by which the world has been crucified unto to me, and I unto the world (Galatians 6:14).’ Amen.”

I HAVE FOUND IT![18]

I have found, yes, I have found the wealth of the Divine Name's gem.

My true guru gave me a priceless thing. With his grace, I accepted it.

I found the capital of my several births; I have lost the whole rest of the world.

No one can spend it, no one can steal it. Day by day it increases one and a quarter times.

On the boat of truth, the boatman was my true guru. I came across the ocean of existence.

Mira's Lord is the Mountain-Holder, the suave lover, of whom I merrily, merrily sing.

---

[18] By Mirabai

THE LIVING FLAME OF LOVE[19]

O flame of living love

that wounds with such tenderness

the deep, deepest center of my soul,

now that you have come to me,

conclude, if you so wish,

and rend the fabric of this sweet encounter.

Oh, so gentle the searing!

Oh, so delicate the wound!

Oh, sweet the hand, oh, soft so soft the blow

that tastes of life eternal

and pays each and every debt!

---

[19] This poem by Saint John of the Cross was translated by Edith Grossman

By killing, you have changed death into life.

Oh burning lamps of fire

in whose brilliant, searing light

the inmost caves and caverns of our senses,

which once were dark and blind,

now offer their heat and light

and give an unknown joy to their beloved!

How peaceful and how loving

you waken on my bosom

where you alone do dwell so secretly;

and with your perfumed breath,

so filled with good and glory,

how delicately you show your love to me.

CHILDHOOD[20]

"For what do. I wish to say, Lord, except that I do not know from where I came into what I call this dying life, or living death; I do not know. But the consolation of Your mercies uplifted me, as I heard from the father and mother of my flesh, out of whom and in whom You formed me at the appropriate time, for I do not remember it myself. I was embraced by the comforts of human milk, but neither my mother nor my nurses filled their own breasts for me. It was You Who through them gave me the food of my infancy according to Your ordinance and the riches spread throughout the essence of all things. You also granted me to want no more than You gave, and granted that my

[20] From the Confessions(1.6.7) of St. Augustine, translated by Peter Constantine

nurses wanted to give me what You had given them, for they sought to give me, by divine ordination what they had received in abundance from You. But the good that came to me from them was also good for them, though it did not come from them but through them; for from You, O God, come all good things, and from my God is my entire salvation. This I learned only later, when, through all the inner and outer things You bestow, you called to me; for then I only knew how to suckle, content in what was pleasurable and crying at what offended my flesh, and nothing more."

PARADOXES[21]

Nothing in the world

Is as soft, as weak as water;

Nothing else can wear away

The hard, the strong,

And remain unaltered.

Soft overcomes hard,

Weak overcomes strong.

Everybody knows it,

Nobody uses the knowledge

So the wise say:

By bearing common defilements

---

[21] From the Tao Te Ching translated by Ursula LeGuin

You become a sacrifice at the altar of earth;

By bearing common evils

You become a lord of the world.

Right words sound wrong

EXCERPT FROM THE CULAMALUKYA SUTTA

At one time the Buddha was staying near Sāvatthī in Jeta's Grove, Anāthapiṇḍika's monastery.

Then as Venerable Māluṅkya was in private retreat this thought came to his mind:

"There are several convictions that the Buddha has left undeclared; he has set them aside and refused to comment on them. For example: the cosmos is eternal, or not eternal, or finite, or infinite; the soul and the body are the same thing, or they are different things; after death, a Realized One exists, or doesn't exist, or both exists and doesn't exist, or neither exists nor doesn't exist. The Buddha does not give me a straight answer on these points. I don't like that, and do not accept it. I'll go to him and ask him about this. If he gives me a straight answer on any of these points, I will lead the spiritual life under him. If he does not give me a straight answer on any of these points, I shall resign the training and return to a lesser life."

Then in the late afternoon, Māluṅkya came out of retreat and went to the Buddha. He bowed, sat down to one side, and told the Buddha of his thoughts. He then continued:

"If the Buddha knows that the cosmos is eternal, please tell me. If you know that the cosmos is not eternal, tell me. If you don't know whether the cosmos is eternal or not, then it is straightforward to simply say: 'I neither know nor see.' If you know that the world is finite, or infinite; that the soul and the body are the same thing, or they are different things; that after death, a Realized One exists, or doesn't exist, or both exists and doesn't exist, or neither exists nor doesn't exist, please tell me. If you don't know any of these things, then it is straightforward to simply say: 'I neither know nor see.'"

"What, Māluṅkyaputta, did I ever say to you: 'Come, Māluṅkyaputta, lead the spiritual life under me, and I will declare these things to you'?"

"No, sir."

"Or did you ever say to me: 'Sir, I will lead the spiritual life under the Buddha, and the Buddha will declare these things to me'?"

"No, sir."

"So, it seems that I did not say to you: 'Come, Māluṅkyaputta, lead the spiritual life under me, and I will declare these things to you.' And you never said to me: 'Sir, I will lead the spiritual life under the Buddha, and the Buddha will declare these things to me.' In that case, you silly man, are you really in a position to be abandoning anything?

Suppose someone were to say this: 'I will not lead the spiritual life under the Buddha until the Buddha declares to me that the cosmos is eternal, or that the cosmos is not eternal ... or that after death a Realized One neither exists nor doesn't exist.' That would still remain undeclared by the Realized One, and meanwhile that person would die.

Suppose a man was struck by an arrow thickly smeared with poison. His friends and colleagues, relatives and kin would get a field surgeon to treat him. But the man would say: 'I won't pull out this arrow as long as I don't know whether the man who wounded me was an aristocrat, a brahmin, a peasant, or a menial.' He'd say: 'I won't pull out this arrow as long as I don't know the following things about the man who wounded me: his name and clan; whether he's tall, short, or medium; whether his skin is black, brown, or tawny; and what village, town, or city he comes from. I won't pull out this arrow as long as I don't know whether the bow that wounded me is made of wood or cane; whether the bow-string is made of swallow-wort fibre, sunn hemp fibre, sinew, sanseveria fibre, or spurge fibre; whether the shaft is made from a bush or a plantation tree; whether the shaft was fitted with feathers from a vulture, a heron, a hawk, a peacock, or a stork; whether the shaft was bound with sinews of a cow, a buffalo, a swamp deer, or a gibbon; and whether the arrowhead was spiked, razor-tipped, barbed, made of iron or a calf's tooth, or lancet-shaped.' That man would still not have learned these things, and meanwhile they'd die.

In the same way, suppose someone was to say: 'I will not lead the spiritual life under the Buddha until the Buddha declares to me that the cosmos is eternal, or that the cosmos is not eternal … or that after death a Realized One neither exists nor doesn't exist.' That would still remain undeclared by the Realized One, and meanwhile that person would die.

It's not true that if there were the view 'the cosmos is eternal' there would be the living of the spiritual life. It's not true that if there were the view 'the cosmos is not eternal' there would be the living of the spiritual life. When there is the view that the cosmos is eternal or that the cosmos is not eternal, there is rebirth, there is old age, there is death, and there is sorrow, lamentation, pain, sadness, and distress. And it is the defeat of these things in this very life that I advocate. It's not true that if there were the view 'the world is finite' … 'the world is infinite' … 'the soul and the body are the same thing' … 'the soul and the body are different things' … 'a Realized One exists after death' … 'a Realized One doesn't exist after death' … 'a Realized One both exists and doesn't exist after death' … 'a Realized One neither exists nor doesn't exist after death' there would be the living of the spiritual life. When there are any of these views there is rebirth, there is old age, there is death, and there is sorrow, lamentation, pain, sadness, and distress. And it is the defeat of these things in this very life that I advocate.

So, Māluṅkyaputta, you should remember what I have not declared as undeclared, and what I have declared as declared. And what have I not declared? I have not declared the following: 'the cosmos is eternal,' 'the cosmos is not eternal,' 'the world is finite,' 'the world is infinite,' 'the soul and the body are the same thing,' 'the soul and the body are different things,' 'a Realized One exists after death,' 'a Realized One doesn't exist after death,' 'a Realized One both exists and doesn't exist after death,' 'a Realized One neither exists nor doesn't exist after death.'

And why haven't I declared these things? Because they aren't beneficial or relevant to the fundamentals of the spiritual life. They don't lead to disillusionment, dispassion, cessation, peace, insight, awakening, and extinguishment. That's why I haven't declared them.

And what have I declared? I have declared the following: 'this is suffering,' ‘this is the origin of suffering,’ ‘this is the cessation of suffering,’ ‘this is the practice that leads to the cessation of suffering.’

And why have I declared these things? Because they are beneficial and relevant to the fundamentals of the spiritual life. They lead to disillusionment, dispassion, cessation, peace, insight, awakening, and extinguishment. That’s why I have declared them. So, Māluṅkyaputta, you should remember what I have not declared as undeclared, and what I have declared as declared.”

That is what the Buddha said. Satisfied, Venerable Māluṅkyaputta was happy with what the Buddha said.

THE SNAKE THAT REFUSED TO HISS

Ramakrishna narrated this story saying, "A man living in society should make a show of tamas[22] to protect himself from evil-minded people. But he should not harm anybody in anticipation of harm likely to be done to him."

Some cowherd boys used to tend their cows in a meadow where a terrible poisonous snake lived. Everyone was on the alert for fear of it. One day a brahmachari[23] was going along the meadow. The boys ran to him and said, 'Revered sir, please don't go that way. A venomous snake lives over there.' 'What of it, my good children?' said the brahmachari. 'I am not afraid of the snake. I know some mantras.' So saying,

---

[22] In this context, Tamas means violence

[23] A celibate monk

he continued on his way along the meadow. But the cowherd boys, being afraid, did not accompany him. In the meantime, the snake moved swiftly toward him with an upraised hood. As soon as it came near, he recited a mantra, and the snake lay at his feet like an earthworm. The brahmachari said: 'Look here. Why do you go about doing harm? Come, I will give you a holy word. By repeating it you will learn to love God. Ultimately you will realize Him and so get rid of your violent nature.' Saying this, he taught the snake a holy word and initiated him into spiritual life. The snake bowed before the teacher and said, 'Revered sir, how shall I practice spiritual discipline?'

'Repeat that sacred word', said the teacher, 'and do no harm to anybody.' As he was about to depart, the brahmachari said, 'I shall see you again.'

Some days passed and the cowherd boys noticed that the snake would not bite. They threw stones at it. Still, it showed no anger; it behaved as if it were an earthworm. One day one of the boys came close to it, caught it by the tail, and, whirling it round and round, dashed it again and again on the ground and threw it away. The snake vomited blood and became unconscious. It was stunned. It could not move. So, thinking it dead, the boys went their way.

"Late at night the snake regained consciousness. Slowly and with great difficulty it dragged itself into its hole; its bones were broken, and it could scarcely move. Many days passed. The snake became a mere skeleton covered with a skin. Now and then, at night, it would come out in search of food. For fear of the boys, it would not leave its hole during the day-time. Since receiving the sacred word from the teacher, it had given up doing harm to others. It maintained its life on dirt, leaves, or the fruit that dropped from the trees.

"About a year later the brahmachari came that way again and asked after the snake. The cowherd boys told him that it was dead. But he couldn't believe them. He knew that the snake would not die before attaining the fruit of the holy word with which it had been initiated. He found his way to the place and, searching here and there, called it by the name he had given it. Hearing the teacher's voice, it came out of its hole and bowed before him with great reverence. 'How are you?' asked the brahmachari. 'I am well, sir', replied the snake. 'But', the teacher asked, 'why are you so thin?' The snake replied: 'Revered sir, you ordered me not to harm anybody. So, I have been living only on leaves and fruit. Perhaps that has made me thinner.'

"The snake had developed the quality of Sattva; it could not be angry with anyone. It had totally forgotten that the cowherd boys had almost killed it.

"The brahmachari said: 'It can't be mere want of food that has reduced you to this state. There must be some other reason. Think a little.' Then the snake remembered that the boys had dashed it against the ground. It said: 'Yes, revered sir, now I remember. The boys one day dashed me violently against the ground. They are ignorant, after all. They didn't realize what a great change had come over my mind. How could they know I wouldn't bite or harm anyone?' The brahmachari exclaimed: 'What a shame! You are such a fool! You don't know how to protect yourself. I asked you not to bite, but I didn't forbid you to hiss. Why didn't you scare them by hissing?'

MY MIND HAS TAKEN TO LIVING FREE[24]

Oh friend, my mind has

taken to living free!

The joy of remembering the Lord

Cannot be found in plenty

My mind rejoices in poverty

My mind rejoices in simplicity

My mind has taken to living free!

[24] This poem by Kabir was translated by Vipul Rikhi and Shabnam Virmani

A bowl and a staff is all I carry

Yet my kingdom stretches wherever I see

My mind has taken to living free!

Praise or abuse, listen to it all

But don't stray from simplicity

My mind has taken to living free!

My dwelling in the city of love

Became beautiful with patience

My mind has taken to living free!

Your body will bite the dust one day

Why strut about, so smug, so vain?

My mind has taken to living free!

Says Kabir, listen seekers

The Lord is found in contentment

My mind has taken to living free!

GOD'S LOVE JUSTIFIES BEGGING[25]

In the mind of St. Francis, begging alms for the love of the Lord God was a very noble, worthy and gentlemanly thing to do, both in the eyes of God and according to worldly judgement. He reasoned that after mankind had fallen into sin, all the things the heavenly Father had created for man's use were given to both worthy and unworthy men gratuitously as alms, because of his love for his beloved Son. So, as St. Francis used to say, a servant of God should beg alms for the love of the Lord more willingly and gladly than a courtly gentleman taking pleasure in his generosity. In making a purchase he says, "Give me this penny's worth of

[25] From *We Were with Saint Francis* by Salvator Butler

goods and I shall give you a hundred pieces of silver for it." The servant of God gives a thousandfold more than he receives because what he offers is the love of God, and this is what a man gains in return for the alms he gives. Compared to God's love, all things on earth are as nothing — and even the things of heaven.

Before the brothers had begun to increase in numbers, and also after they had become numerous, St. Francis would journey about preaching. He went to preach in many cities and castle towns where the brothers did not yet have places. Sometimes a wealthy nobleman would invite him reverently to accept his hospitality and dine with him in his home. Even though the holy father knew that his host had prepared plentifully for his bodily needs, he would go begging at mealtime so as to assure a good example for the brothers, and so as to honor the nobility and dignity of Lady Poverty.

It was a usual thing for him to say to his host, "I won't renounce my royal dignity[26], my heritage, my vocation, and the vows I and the other Lesser Brothers have made. I'm going out to beg for alms. It may be that I'll come back with no more than a few scraps, but I shall have fulfilled my duty." Thus, against the wishes of his host, he would go out begging, and the host would go along with him. On returning, his host would take the alms that had been given to St. Francis and keep them, cherishing them as relics. The one who writes this has often seen such things happen and gives testimony thereto.

---

[26] By 'royal dignity', St. Francis refers God and Lady Poverty.

THE DHAMMAPADA ON CRAVING[27]

When a person lives heedlessly,

his craving grows like a creeping vine.

He runs now here

and now there,

as if looking for a fruit: a monkey in a forest.

If this sticky, uncouth craving

overcomes you in the world,

your sorrows grow like wild grass

after rain.

If, in the world, you overcome

this uncouth craving, hard to escape,

---

[27] Translated by Thanissaro Bhiku

sorrows roll off you

like water beads off a lotus.

To all of you gathered here

I say: good fortune.

Dig up craving

— as when seeking medicinal roots, wild grass — by the root.

...

If craving-obsession

is not rooted out,

this suffering returns

again and again.

...

Encircled with craving,

people hop round and around

like a rabbit caught in a snare.

A monk should dispel craving,

should aspire to dispassion for himself.

Cleared of the underbrush

but obsessed with the forest,

set free from the forest,

right back to the forest he runs.

Come, see the person set free

who runs right back to the same old chains!

That's not a strong bond

— so say the enlightened —

the one made of iron, of wood, or of grass.

To be smitten, enthralled,

with jewels and ornaments,

longing for children and wives:

that's the strong bond

— so say the enlightened —

one that's constraining,

elastic,

hard to untie.

But having cut it, they

— the enlightened — go forth

free of longing, abandoning sensual ease.

All suffering and stress.

Gone to the beyond of becoming

you let go of in front,

let go of behind

let go of between

With a heart everywhere released,

you don't come again to birth

and aging ...

Riches ruin the man weak in discernment,

but not those who seek the beyond.

Through craving for riches

the man weak in discernment

ruins himself as he would others.

Fields are spoiled by weeds;

people, by passion,

So what's given to those

free of passion

bears great fruit.

Fields are spoiled by weeds,

people, by aversion.

So what’s given to those

free of passion

bears great fruit.

WORK IS WORSHIP[28]

The highest man cannot work, for there is no binding element, no attachment, no ignorance in him. A ship is said to have passed over a mountain of magnet ore, and all the bolts and bars were drawn out, and it went to pieces. It is in ignorance that struggle remains, because we are all really atheists. Real theists cannot work. We are atheists more or less. We do not see God or believe in Him. He is G-O-D to us, and nothing more. There are moments when we think He is near, but then we fall down again. When you see Him, who struggles for whom? Help the Lord! There is a proverb in our language, "Shall we teach the Architect of the universe how to build?" So those are the highest of mankind who do not

[28] From a speech by Swami Vivekananda

work. The next time you see these silly phrases about the world and how we must all help God and do this or that for Him, remember this. Do not think such thoughts; they are too selfish. All the work you do is subjective, is done for your own benefit. God has not fallen into a ditch for you and me to help Him out by building a hospital or something of that sort. He *allows* you to work. He allows you to exercise your muscles in this great gymnasium, not in order to help Him but that you may help yourself. Do you think even an ant will die for want of your help? Most arrant blasphemy! The world does not need you at all. The world goes on, you are like a drop in the ocean. A leaf does not move, the wind does not blow without Him. Blessed are we that we are given the privilege of working for Him, not of helping Him. Cut out this word "help" from your mind. You cannot help; it is blaspheming. You are here yourself at His pleasure. Do you mean to say, you help Him? You worship. When you give a morsel of food to the dog, you worship the dog as God. God is in that dog. He is the dog. He is all and in all. We are allowed to worship Him. Stand in that reverent attitude to the whole universe, and then will come perfect non-attachment. This should be your duty. This is the proper attitude of work. This is the secret taught by Karma Yoga.

ETERNAL LIFE[29]

Eternal Life is gained

by utter abandonment of one's own life.

When God appears to His ardent lover,

the lover is absorbed in Him, and not so much as a hair of the lover remains.

True lovers are as shadows

---

[29] Rumi poem translated by R.A. Nicholson

HOW SAINT FRANCIS TAMED THE WILD TURTLE-DOVES

ONE day, a youth had taken many turtle-doves, and as he was carrying them to sell them, St. Francis, who ever had singular compassion for gentle creatures, chanced to meet him, and looking upon those turtle-doves with compassionate eye, said to the youth: "Good youth, I pray thee give them to me, that birds so gentle, which in the Scriptures are likened unto chaste and humble and faithful souls, come not into the hands of cruel men who would slay them". Whereupon, inspired of God, he forthwith gave them all to St. Francis; and he receiving them in his bosom, began to speak to them sweetly: "O my sisters, simple, innocent, chaste turtle-doves, why do you let yourselves be taken? Now I desire to save you from death and to make nests for you, so that ye may bring forth fruit and multiply, according to the commandments of our Creator." And St. Francis went and made nests for them all, and they resorted thereunto, and began to lay eggs and to hatch forth their young in the presence of the friars; and so tame were they and so familiar with St. Francis and with the other friars that they might have been domestic fowls which had always been fed by them; and never did they depart until St. Francis with his blessing gave them leave to do so. And to the young man, which had given them unto him, St. Francis said: "Son, thou wilt yet be a friar in this Order, and thou wilt serve Jesus Christ with all thy heart"; and so it came to pass, for the said youth became a friar and lived in the Order in great sanctity.

A STORY FROM THE BUDDHA

The Buddha was walking through Deer Park in the holy city of Varanasi, India, when he chanced upon an injured deer. It lay on the ground slowly dying from an arrow wound.

At its side stood two Brahmins, holy men, arguing about the exact time that life leaves the body. It was obvious that they had been arguing for some time and hadn't reached any conclusion. Eager to end the debate, they asked the Buddha for his opinion.

Ignoring them, he approached the deer and slowly pulled out the arrow, saving the animal's life.

EXCERPT FROM THE LIFE OF SAINT THERESA[30]

It happened, also, as time went on, and it happens now from time to time, that our Lord showed me still greater secrets. The soul, even if it would, has neither the means not the power to see more than what He shows it; and so, each time, I saw nothing more than what our Lord was pleased to let me see. But such was the vision, that the least part of it was enough to make my soul amazed, and to raise it so high that it esteems and counts as nothing all the things of this life. I wish I could describe, in some measure, the smallest portion of what I saw; but when I think of doing it, I find it impossible; for the mere difference alone between the light we have here below, and that which is seen in a vision

[30] Translated by David Lewis

— both being light — is so great, that there is no comparison between them; the brightness of the sun itself seems to be something exceedingly loathsome. In a word, the imagination, however strong it may be, can neither conceive nor picture to itself this light, nor any one of the things which our Lord showed me in a joy so supreme that it cannot be described; for then all the senses exult so deeply and so sweetly that no description is possible; and so it is better to say nothing more.

I was in this state once for more than an hour, our Lord showing me wonderful things. He seemed as if He would not leave me. He said to me, "See, My daughter, what they lose who are against Me; do not fail to tell them of it." Ah, my Lord, how little good my words will do them, who are made blind by their own conduct, if Thy Majesty will not give them light! Some, to whom Thou hast given it, there are, who have profited by the knowledge of Thy greatness; but as they see it revealed to one so wicked and base as I am, I look upon it as a great thing if there should be any found to believe me. Blessed be Thy name, and blessed be Thy compassion; for I can trace, at least in my own soul, a visible improvement. Afterwards I wished I had continued in that trance for ever, and that I had not returned to consciousness, because of an abiding sense of contempt for everything here below; all seemed to be filth; and I see how meanly we employ ourselves who are detained on earth.

...A soul in this state attains to a certain freedom, which is so complete that none can understand it who does not possess it. It is a real and true detachment, independent of our efforts;

God effects it all Himself; for His Majesty reveals the truth in such a way, that it remains so deeply impressed on our souls as to make it clear that we of ourselves could not thus acquire it in so short a time.

...It seems to me, also, that the rapture was a great help to recognize our true home, and to see that we are pilgrims here; it is a great thing to see what is going on there and to know where we have to live; for if a person has to go and settle in another country, it is a great help to him, in undergoing the fatigues of his journey, that he has discovered it to be a country where he may live in the most perfect peace. Moreover, it makes it easy for us to think of the things of heaven, and to have our conversation there. It is a great gain, because the mere looking up to heaven makes the soul recollected; for as our Lord has been pleased to reveal heaven in some degree, my soul dwells upon it in thought; and it happens occasionally that they who are about me, and with whom I find consolation, are those whom I know to be living in heaven, and that I look upon them only as really alive; while those who are on earth are so dead, that the whole world seems unable to furnish me with companions, particularly when these impetuosities of love are upon me. Everything seems a dream, and what I see with the bodily eyes an illusion. What I have seen with the eyes of the soul is that which my soul desires; and as it finds itself far away from those things, that is death.

In a word, it is a very great mercy which our Lord gives to that soul to which He grants the like visions, for they help it in much, and also in carrying a heavy cross, since nothing satisfies it, and everything is against it; and if our Lord did not now and then suffer these visions to be forgotten, though they recur again and again to the memory, I know not how life could be borne. May He be blessed and praised for ever and ever!

I SEE SO DEEPLY WITHIN MYSELF[31]

I see so deeply within myself.

Not needing my eyes, I can see
everything clearly.

Why would I want to bother my eyes
again

Now that I see the world through His
eyes?

[31] Poem by Rumi

CREATION[32]

We can see all those things which Thou hast made because they are — but they are because Thou seest them. And we see with our eyes that they are, and we see with our minds that they are good. But Thou sawest them as made when Thou sawest that they would be made. And now, in this present time, we have been moved to do well, now that our heart has been quickened by thy Spirit; but in the former time, having forsaken Thee, we were moved to do evil. But Thou, O the one good God, hast never ceased to do good! And we have accomplished certain good works by thy good gifts, and even though they are not eternal, still we hope, after these things here, to find our rest in thy great

---

[32] From the Confessions of St. Augustine translated by Albert C. Outler

sanctification. But Thou art the Good, and needest no rest, and art always at rest, because Thou thyself art thy own rest. What man will teach men to understand this? And what angel will teach the angels? Or what angels will teach men? We must ask it of Thee; we must seek it in Thee; we must knock for it at thy door. Only thus shall we receive; only thus shall we find; only thus shall thy door be opened.

FOR HUNGER[33]

For hunger,

there is the town's rice in the begging bowl.

For thirst

there are tanks, streams wells.

For sleep

there are the ruins of temples.

For soul's

company

I have you, O lord white as jasmine.

---

[33] This poem by Mahadeviyakka was translated by AK Ramanujan

THE VALUE OF ADVERSITY[34]

It is good for us to have trials and troubles at times, for they often remind us that we are on probation and ought not to hope in any worldly thing. It is good for us sometimes to suffer contradiction, to be misjudged by men even though we do well and mean well. These things help us to be humble and shield us from vainglory. When to all outward appearances men give us no credit, when they do not think well of us, then we are more inclined to seek God Who sees our hearts. Therefore, a man ought to root himself so firmly in God that he will not need the consolations of men.

When a man of good will is afflicted, tempted, and tormented by evil

---

[34] From The Imitation of Christ translated by Aloysius Croft and Harold Bolton

thoughts, he realizes clearly that his greatest need is God, without Whom he can do no good. Saddened by his miseries and sufferings, he laments and prays. He wearies of living longer and wishes for death that he might be dissolved and be with Christ. Then he understands fully that perfect security and complete peace cannot be found on earth.

ANY SOUL THAT DRANK THE NECTAR[35]

Any soul that drank the nectar of your passion was lifted.

From that water of life he is in a state of elation.

Death came, smelled me, and sensed your fragrance instead.

From then on, death lost all hope of me.

[35] By Rumi

A POTTED PLANT[36]

I pull a sun from my coin purse each day.

And at night I let my pet, the moon,

Run freely into the sky meadow.

If I whistled,

She would turn her head and look at me.

If I then waved my arms,

She would come back wagging a marvelous tail

Of stars.

There are always a few men like me

In this world

Who are house-sitting for God.

---

[36] This Hafiz poem was translated by Daniel Ladinsky

We share His royal duties:

I water each day a favorite potted plant

Of His —

This earth.

Ask the Friend for love.

Ask Him again.

For I have learned that every heart will get

What it prays for

Most.

PURITY OF MIND AND UNITY OF PURPOSE[37]

A man is raised up from the earth by two wings—simplicity and purity. There must be simplicity in his intention and purity in his desires. Simplicity leads to God, purity embraces and enjoys Him.

If your heart is free from ill-ordered affection, no good deed will be difficult for you. If you aim at and seek after nothing but the pleasure of God and the welfare of your neighbor, you will enjoy freedom within.

If your heart were right, then every created thing would be a mirror of life for you and a book of holy teaching, for there is no creature so small and worthless that it does not show forth

---

[37] From *The Imitation of Christ* translated by Aloysius Croft and Harold Bolton

the goodness of God. If inwardly you were good and pure, you would see all things clearly and understand them rightly, for a pure heart penetrates to heaven and hell, and as a man is within, so he judges what is without. If there be joy in the world, the pure of heart certainly possess it; and if there be anguish and affliction anywhere, an evil conscience knows it too well.

As iron cast into fire loses its rust and becomes glowing white, so he who turns completely to God is stripped of his sluggishness and changed into a new man. When a man begins to grow lax, he fears a little toil and welcomes external comfort, but when he begins perfectly to conquer himself and to walk bravely in the ways of God, then he thinks those things less difficult which he thought so hard before.

A ZEN PARABLE

Yamaoka Tesshu was a young student of Zen. He traveled, visiting one spiritual teacher after another. Eventually, he came upon Dokuon of Shokoku.

Hoping to show his high levels of spiritual attainment, Tesshu said: "All sentient beings are nonexistent, be it you, me, or the Buddha. Everything is empty. There is no enlightenment, no ignorance, no sages, no emotions, no world. Nothing is given and nothing is received."

Dokuon, who was calmly smoking his pipe, was quiet for a moment. Suddenly, he took out a bamboo scroll and whacked Tesshu on the head. "Why did you do that!" Tesshu angrily called out.

"Hmm," Dokuon said, "If nothing exists, from what did this anger come about?"

YOUR SLANDER IS SWEET[38]

Rana, to me your slander is sweet.
Some praise me, some blame me. I
go the other way.
On the narrow path, I found God's
people. What should I turn back for?
I am learning wisdom among the
wise, and the wicked look at me
with malice.
Mira's Lord is Giridhar Nagar[39].
Let the wicked burn in the kitchen fire.
Mira's God is the lifter of mountains.

---

[38] In this poem, Mirabai addresses her father-in-law, Rana

[39] Krishna

I don't like your strange world, Rana,
A world where there are no holy men,
and all the people are trash.
I have given up ornaments, given up
braiding my hair.
I have given up putting on kajal,
and putting my hair up.
Mira's Lord is Giridhar Nagar; I have
found a perfect bridegroom.

THERE IS A CANDLE IN YOUR HEART[40]

There is a candle in the heart of man, waiting to be kindled.

In separation from the Friend, there is a cut waiting to be stitched.

O, you who are ignorant of endurance and the burning fire of love —

Love comes of its own free will, it can't be learned in any school.

[40] A poem by Rumi

PARABLE OF THE THREE ROBBERS[41]

Let me tell you a story. Once a rich man was passing through a forest, when three robbers surrounded him and robbed him of all his wealth. After snatching all his possessions from him, one of the robbers said: 'What's the good of keeping the man alive? Kill him.' Saying this, he was about to strike their victim with his sword, when the second robber interrupted and said: 'There's no use in killing him. Let us bind him fast and leave him here. Then he won't be able to tell the police.' Accordingly the robbers tied him with a rope, left him, and went away.

"After a while the third robber returned to the rich man and said: 'Ah! You're badly hurt, aren't you? Come, I'm going

[41] By Sri Ramakrishna

to release you.' The third robber set the man free and led him out of the forest. When .they came near the highway, the robber said, 'Follow this road and you will reach home easily.''But you must come with me too', said the man. 'You have done so much for me. We shall all be happy to see you at our home.' 'No,' said the robber, 'it is not possible for me to go there. The police will arrest me.' So saying, he left the rich man after pointing out his way.

"Now, the first robber, who said: 'What's the good of keeping the man alive? Kill him', is Tamas[42]. It destroys. The second robber is Rajas[43], which binds a man to the world and entangles him in a variety of activities. Rajas makes him forget

---

[42] The mode of being associated with lethargy and darkness

[43] The mode of being associated with passion and energy

God. Sattva[44] alone shows the way to God. It produces virtues like compassion, righteousness, and devotion. Again, Sattva is like the last step of the stairs. Next to it is the roof. The Supreme Brahman is man's own abode. One cannot attain the Knowledge of Brahman unless one transcends the three gunas[45].

[44] The mode of being associated with truth

[45] Namely Tamas, Rajas, and Sattva

SOULS WITHOUT PRAYER[46]

A short time ago I was told by a very learned man that souls without prayer are like people whose bodies or limbs are paralyzed: they possess feet and hands but they cannot control them. In the same way, there are souls so infirm and so accustomed to busying themselves with outside affairs that nothing can be done for them, and it seems as though they are incapable of entering within themselves at all.

---

[46] From *The Interior Castle* by Saint Theresa by E. Allison Peers

THE WASHERMAN AND THE DONKEY[47]

A washerman visited a village every day. He went to every house in the town, collected all the dirty clothes, loaded them up on his donkey, and set off to the river. After reaching the river, he gasped in horror. He had forgotten the rope at home. He panicked and looked in all directions for some help. Without his rope, he could not tie his donkey to a tree. If the donkey remained untied, it could walk away, and he would lose his livelihood. If he went back to the village, he would not have enough time to return and wash the clothes. He would lose his day's work, which meant he could not earn money to feed the family.

---

[47] The parable from Sri Ramakrishna was narrated by Akshay Om

He was sweating anxiously when a wise man walked up to him and asked him about his troubles. After listening to his story, the wise man smiled and offered the washerman a suggestion.

"Pretend to tie the donkey with a rope and go to the river. The donkey will graze and wait for you here." The washerman was astounded, but because he lacked other options, he tried it out. He took an imaginary rope, wound it around the donkey's neck, and pretended to tie it to a tree.

He walked a few steps and saw that the donkey had begun grazing. He walked all the way to the river, and the donkey had not moved. The washerman spent all day washing his clothes peacefully, dried the clothes, and loaded them back on the donkey. He pats the donkey and signals that they are ready to go, but the donkey does not move. The washerman is puzzled when the wise man appears and reminds the washerman to untie the donkey. The washerman opens the imaginary rope, and the donkey starts trotting off to the village.

DON'T STAY[48]

Don't stay —

the land's a wilderness

This world's a paltry paper packet —

a spot of rain

will wash it away.

The world's a garden of thorns —

snarled and snared,

we'll perish in pain.

This world's all tree and tinder —

kindled it will roast us

like sacrificial victims.

Kabir says, listen my good men,

---

[48] This poem by Kabir was translated by Vinay Dharwadker

the True master’s name

is our lasting abode —

our station, our destination.

SEEK OUT GOD[49]

Many years ago, I visited a great sage of our own country, a very holy man. We talked of our revealed book, the Vedas, of [the] Bible, of the Koran, and of revealed books in general. At the close of our talk, this good man asked me to go to the table and take up a book; it was a book which, among other things, contained a forecast of the rainfall during the year. The sage said, "Read that." And I read out the quantity of rain that was to fall. He said, "Now take the book and squeeze it." I did so and he said, "Why, my boy, not a drop of water comes out. Until the water comes out, it is all book, book. So until your religion makes you realize God, it is useless. He who only studies books for religion reminds one of the fable of the ass

---

[49] From a speech by Swami Vivekananda

which carried a heavy load of sugar on its back, but did not know the sweetness of it."

Shall we advise men to kneel down and cry, "O miserable sinners that we are!" No, rather let us remind them of their divine nature. I will tell you a story. A lioness in search of prey came upon a flock of sheep, and as she jumped at one of them, she gave birth to a cub and died on the spot. The young lion was brought up in the flock, ate grass, and bleated like a sheep, and it never knew that it was a lion. One day a lion came across the flock and was astonished to see in it a huge lion eating grass and bleating like a sheep. At his sight the flock fled and the lion-sheep with them. But the lion watched his opportunity and one day found the lion-sheep asleep. He woke him up and said, "You are a lion." The other said, "No," and began to bleat like a sheep. But the stranger lion took him to a lake and asked him to look in the water at his own image and see if it did not resemble him, the stranger lion. He looked and acknowledged that it did. Then the stranger lion began to roar and asked him to do the same. The lion-sheep tried his voice and was soon roaring as grandly as the other. And he was a sheep no longer.

My friends, I would like to tell you all that you are mighty as lions.

If the room is dark, do you go about beating your chest and crying, "It is dark, dark, dark!" No, the only way to get the light is to strike a light, and then the darkness goes. The only way to realise the light above you is to strike the spiritual light within you, and the darkness of sin and impurity will flee away. Think of your higher self, not of your lower.

PURITY[50]

Tell me, O pandit,

what place is pure —

where can I sit

and eat my meal?

Mother was impure,

father was impure —

the fruits they bore

were also impure.

They arrived impure,

they left impure —

unlucky folks,

they died impure.

---

[50] This Kabir poem was translated by Vinay Dharwadker

My tongue's impure,

my words are impure,

my ears, my eyes,

they're all impure —

you brahmins,

you've stolen the fire

but you can't burn off

the impurity of the senses!

The fire, too, is impure,

the water's impure —

so even the kitchen's

nothing but impure.

The ladle's impure

that serves a meal,

and they're impure

who sit and eat their fill.

Cowdung's impure,

the bathing-square's impure —

it's very curbs

are nothing but impure.

Kabir says,

only they are pure

who've completely cleansed their thinking.

THE BEAUTIFUL SERMON WHICH FRIAR RUFFINO AND ST. FRANCIS OF ASSISI PREACHED NAKED[51]

Through continual contemplation, Friar Ruffino was so absorbed in God that he had become well-nigh insensible and dumb, and exceeding rarely spoke; and moreover he had neither grace nor courage nor eloquence in preaching. Nevertheless St. Francis, one day, ordered him to go to Assisi and preach to the people that which God inspired him to preach. Whereto Friar Ruffino made answer: "Reverend father, I beseech thee that thou have me excused and send me not, because, as thou knowest, I have not the gift of preaching and am a simple man and ignorant". Then said St. Francis:

[51] From *Little Flowers of Saint Francis*

"Inasmuch as thou hast not obeyed at once, I command thee by holy obedience that thou go to Assisi, naked as thou wast born, save only for thy breeches, and that thou enter into a church, thus naked, and preach to the people". At this command, the aforesaid Friar Ruffino stripped himself, and went to Assisi, and entered into a church; and, when he had bowed himself before the altar, he went up into the pulpit and began to preach; whereat children and men began to laugh, and said: "Behold, now, how these men do so much penance that they become fools and beside themselves". In the meantime, St. Francis, considering the prompt obedience of Friar Ruffino, who was of one of the noblest families of Assisi, and of the hard commandment which he had given him, began to blame himself, saying: "How hast thou such great presumption, son of Peter Bernardoni, vile manikin, as to command Friar Ruffino, one of the first gentlemen of Assisi, to go naked to preach to the people like a madman? By God, thou shalt prove in thine own person that which thou orderest others to do." And anon, in fervour of spirit, he stripped himself naked likewise, and so gat him up to Assisi, taking with him Friar Leo, that he might carry his habit and that of Friar Ruffino. And, when the men of Assisi beheld St. Francis likewise naked they made a mock at him, deeming that he and Friar Ruffino had gone mad through excessive penance. Then St. Francis entered into the church where Friar Ruffino was preaching these words: "Oh most dearly beloved, flee the world and cease from sin; render unto others that which is theirs, if ye would escape hell; keep the commandments of God, loving God and your neighbour if ye would go to heaven; do penance if ye would possess the kingdom of heaven". Thereupon St. Francis went up naked into the pulpit, and began to preach so marvellously of the contempt of the world, of holy repentance, of voluntary poverty and of the desire of the celestial kingdom, and of the nakedness and shame of the passion of our Lord Jesus Christ, that all they which were at the sermon, men and women in great numbers, began to weep very bitterly, with wonderful devotion and compunction of heart; and not there alone, but throughout the whole of Assisi, was there on that day so great weeping for the passion of Christ that never had there been the like; and, the people being thus edified and comforted by the work of St. Francis and Friar Ruffino, St. Francis reclothed Friar Ruffino and himself; and, thus reclothed, they returned to the Place of the Porziuncula praising and glorifying

God who had given them grace to conquer themselves through contempt of self, and to edify the little sheep of Christ by their good example, and to show how much the world is to be despised. And on that day so greatly did the devotion of the people increase toward them, that he who might touch the hem of their garment deemed himself blessed.

YOU ARE STILL CARRYING HER!

A senior monk and a junior monk were traveling through a forest. As they prepared to ford a fast-flowing river, they noticed a beautiful young woman trying to cross. She asked them if they could carry her across.

The monks exchanged glances: they had both taken vows not to touch women.

Without saying anything, the senior monk picked up the woman, placed her on his shoulders, and carried her to the other side. He placed her gently on the ground and continued on his journey.

The junior monk was speechless. Several hours passed in silence.

Finally, the monk blurted out: "Why did you touch that woman? Do you not remember our vows?"

The older monk responded: "Brother, I let go of her on the other side of the river two hours ago. It looks like you are still carrying her."

THE DAGGER OF LOVE[52]

The dagger of love has pierced my heart.

I was going to the river to fetch water,

A golden pitcher on my head.

Hari[53] has bound me

By the thin thread of love,

And wherever He draws me,

Thither I go.

Mira's Lord is the courtly Giridhara:

This is the nature

Of his dark and beautiful form.

---

[52] A poem by Mirabai

[53] Hari and Giridhara are names of Krishna, a Hindu deity.

THE SOUL SUFFERS LONGING FOR GOD[54]

I live, but not in myself, and I have such hope that I die because I do not die.

I no longer live within myself and I cannot live without God, for having neither him nor myself what will life be? It will be a thousand deaths, longing for my true life and dying because I do not die.

This life that I live is no life at all, and so I die continually until I live with you; hear me, my God: I do not desire this life, I am dying because I do not die.

When I am away from you what life can I have except to endure the bitterest death known? I pity myself, for I go on

[54] By Saint John of the Cross

and on living, dying because I do not die.

A fish that leaves the water has this relief: the dying it endures ends at last in death. What death can equal my pitiable life? For the longer I live, the more drawn out is my dying.

When I try to find relief seeing you in the Sacrament, I find this greater sorrow: I cannot enjoy you wholly. All things are affliction since I do not see you as I desire, and I die because I do not die.

And if I rejoice, Lord, in the hope of seeing you, yet seeing I can lose you doubles my sorrow. Living in such fear and hoping as I hope, I die because I do not die.

Lift me from this death, my God, and give me life; do not hold me bound with these bonds so strong; see how I long to see you; my wretchedness is so complete that I die because I do not die.

I will cry out for death and mourn my living while I am held here for my sins. O my God, when will it be that I can truly say: now I live because I do not die?

LETTER BY FRANK LAUBACH[55]

Tonight, lonesome and half ill with a cold, I am learning from experience that there is a deep peace that grows out of illness and loneliness and a sense of failure. These things do drive me up my hill to God, and there comes into my soul through the very tears a comfort which is so much better than laughter. It is "the peace of God that passeth all understanding" unless one has it. God cannot get close when everything is delightful. He seems to need these darker hours, these empty-hearted hours to mean the most to people. You and I have known that over the coffin. We have known it when we parted and our hearts were sore. We have known it when we lay in bed helpless. Is this a

[55] From *Letters by a Modern Mystic* by Frank C. Laubach.

deep truth in the very heart of nature? We sing, “Nearer, my God, nearer to Thee! E’vn thought it be a cross that raiseth me.” Is the cross the only doorway to the very heart of God?

YOUR CUP OVERFLOWS

A university professor, hoping to learn about Zen, visited Nan-in, a Japanese spiritual master.

Nan-in poured the professor a steaming hot cup of tea. He continued to pour even after the cup overflowed.

"It's overflowing! Stop Pouring!" the professor exclaimed.

Nan-in responded: "Just like this cup, you are full with your own ideas and opinions. How can I teach you Zen unless you first empty out your cup?"

A GREAT YOGI[56]

In my travels I spent time with a great yogi.

Once he said to me.

"Become so still you hear the blood flowing

through your veins."

One night as I sat in quiet,

I seemed on the verge of entering a world inside so vast

I know it is the source of

all of

us.

[56] By Mirabai

THE BLIND MEN AND THE ELEPHANT[57]

Once some blind men chanced to come near an animal that someone told them was an elephant. They were asked what the elephant was like. The blind men began to feel its body. One of them said the elephant was like a pillar; he had touched only its leg. Another said it was like a winnowing-fan; he had touched only its ear.

In this way the others, having touched its tail or belly, gave their different versions of the elephant. Just so, a man who has seen only one aspect of God limits God to that alone. It is his conviction that God cannot be anything else.

---

[57] A parable from Sri Ramakrishna

RELIGION IS REALIZATION[58]

The greatest name man ever gave to God is Truth. Truth is the fruit of realization; therefore seek it within the soul. Get away from all books and forms and let your soul see its Self. "We are deluded and maddened by books", Sri Krishna declares. Be beyond the dualities of nature. The moment you think creed and form and ceremony the "be-all" and "end-all", then you are in bondage. Take part in them to help others, but take care they do not become a bondage. Religion is one, but its application must be various. Let each one, therefore, give his message; but find not the defects in other religions. You must come out from all form if you would see the Light. Drink deep of the nectar of the knowledge of God. The

---

[58] From Swami Vivekananda

man who realizes, "I am He", though clad in rags, is happy. Go forth into the Eternal and come back with eternal energy. The slave goes out to search for truth; he comes back free.

SAINT FRANCIS CONVERTS THE WOLF OF AGOBIO[59]

During the time that St. Francis dwelt in the city of Agobio, there appeared in the territory of Agobio a very great wolf, terrible and fierce, the which not only devoured animals but also men and women, so that all the citizens stood in great fear, because ofttimes he came nigh unto the city; and all men went armed when they went forth from the city, as if they were going to battle; and therewithal they were not able to defend themselves from him, when haply any man encountered him alone; and for dread of this wolf things came to such a pass that no one dared to leave the city. Wherefore, St. Francis, having compassion on the men of the city, was minded to go forth to meet this wolf,

[59] From *Little Flowers of Saint Francis*

albeit the citizens altogether counselled him not to do so; and, making the sign of the cross, he went forth from the city with his companions, putting all his trust in God. And because the others feared to go farther, St. Francis alone took the road toward the place where the wolf was. And lo! while many citizens who had come out to behold this miracle were looking on, the said wolf made at St. Francis with open mouth. Whereupon St. Francis advanced towards him, and making over him the sign of the most holy Cross, called him unto him and spoke to him after this manner: "Come hither, friar wolf. I command thee in Christ's name that thou do no harm to me nor to any other." O marvelous thing! Scarcely had St. Francis made the sign of the cross than the terrible wolf instantly closed his mouth and stayed his running; and, in obedience to that command, came, gentle as a lamb, and laid himself down at the feet of St. Francis. Then St. Francis spoke unto him thus: "Friar wolf, thou dost much damage in these parts, and thou hast committed great crimes, destroying and slaying the creatures of God without His license: and not only hast thou slain and devoured beasts, but thou hast also had the hardihood to slay men, made in the image of God; for the which cause thou dost merit the gallows as a thief and most iniquitous murderer; and all men cry out against thee and complain, and all this city is thine enemy. But I desire, friar wolf, to make peace between thee and them; to the end that thou mayest no more offend them and that they may forgive thee all thy past offences and neither men nor dogs may pursue thee any more." At these words, the wolf, by movements of his body and tail and eyes, and by bowing his head, showed that he accepted that which St. Francis said and was minded to observe the same. Thereupon St. Francis spoke unto him again saying: "Friar wolf, inasmuch as it seems good unto thee to make and keep this peace, I promise thee that, so long as thou shalt live, I will cause thy food to be given thee continually by the men of this city, so that thou shalt no more suffer hunger; for I know full well that whatever of evil thou hast done thou hast done it through hunger. But seeing that I beg for thee this grace, I desire, friar wolf, that thou shouldst promise me that never from henceforward wilt thou injure any human being or any animal. Dost thou promise me this?" And the wolf, by bowing his head, gave evident token that he promised it. And St. Francis said: "Friar wolf, I desire that thou swear me fealty touching this promise, to the end that I may trust thee utterly". Then St. Francis held forth his hand to receive his fealty, and the wolf lifted up his right fore-foot and put it with friendly confidence in the hand of St. Francis, giving thereby such token of fealty as he was able. Thereupon St. Francis said: "Friar wolf, I command thee in the name of Jesus Christ to come now with me, nothing doubting, and let us go and stablish this peace in the name of God". And the wolf went with him obediently, like a gentle lamb; wherefore the citizens beholding the same marvelled greatly. And anon, the fame thereof was noised abroad through all the city, and all the people, men and women, great and small, young and old, thronged to the piazza to see the wolf with St. Francis. And when all the folk were gathered together, St. Francis rose up to preach unto them, saying, among other things, how, by reason of sin, God permits such pestilences; and far more perilous is the fire of hell, the which must for ever torment the damned, than is the fury of a wolf which can only kill the body; how much then are the jaws of hell to be feared when the jaws of a little beast can hold so great a multitude in fear! "Turn ye then, most dear ones, turn ye to God, and do befitting penance for your sins, and God will save you from the wolf in this present world and from the fire of hell in that which is to come". And when he had done preaching, St. Francis said: "Hear ye, my brethren. Friar wolf, who is here before you, hath promised and sworn fealty to me, that he will make peace with you and never more offend you in anything; do ye now promise him to give him every day that whereof he hath need; and I become surety unto you for him that he will faithfully observe this covenant of peace." Then all the people with one voice promised to provide him food continually, and St. Francis spake unto the wolf before them all, saying: "And thou, friar wolf, dost thou promise to observe the covenant of peace which thou hast made with this folk, that thou wilt offend neither men nor beast nor any creature?" And the wolf kneeled him down and bowed his head, and, with gentle movements of his body and tail and ears, showed as far as he was able his determination to keep that covenant wholly. Said St. Francis: "Friar wolf, as thou didst me fealty touching this promise, without the gate, so now I desire that thou do me fealty, before all the people, touching thy promise, and that thou wilt not deceive me concerning my promise and surety which I have given for thee". Then the wolf, lifting up his right foot, put it in the hand of St. Francis. By which act, and by the other acts aforesaid, all the people were fulfilled with so great joy and wonder, alike for devotion toward the saint, and for the strangeness of the miracle, and for the peace with the wolf, that they all began to shout to heaven, praising and blessing God who had sent them St. Francis, who, by his merits, had freed them from the jaws of the cruel beast. And thereafter, the said wolf lived two years in Agobio, and entered familiarly into the houses, going from door to door, neither doing injury to any one nor receiving any; and he was courteously nourished by the people; and, as he thus went through the town and through the houses, never did any dog bark after him. Finally, after two years, friar wolf died of old age; whereat the citizens lamented much, because as long as they saw him going so gently through their city, they recalled the better the virtue and sanctity of St. Francis.

THE DANGERS OF WORLDLY LIFE[60]

God and His glory — this universe is His glory. People see His glory and forget everything. They do not seek God, whose glory is this world. All seek to enjoy 'woman and gold'. But there is too much misery and worry in that. This world is like the whirlpool of the Visalakshi[61]. Once a boat gets into it there is no hope of its rescue. Again, the world is like a thorny bush: you have hardly freed yourself from one set of thorns before you find yourself entangled in another. Once you enter a labyrinth you find it very difficult to get out. Living in the world, a man becomes seared, as it were.

---

[60] From the Gospel of Sri Ramakrishna

[61] A female Hindu deity

I AM MAD WITH LOVE[62]

I am mad with love

And no one understands my plight.

Only the wounded

Understand the agonies of the wounded,

When the fire rages in the heart.

Only the jeweler knows the value of the jewel,

Not the one who lets it go.

In pain I wander from door to door,

But could not find a doctor.

Says Mira: Harken, my Master,

Mira's pain will subside

---

[62] A poem by Mirabai

When Shyam[63] comes as the doctor.

[63] Krishna

THE UNITY OF RELIGION[64]

Through the vistas of the past the voice of the centuries is coming down to us; the voice of the sages of the Himalayas and the recluses of the forest; the voice that came to the Semitic races; the voice that spoke through Buddha and other spiritual giants; the voice that comes from those who live in the light that accompanied man in the beginning of the earth—the light that shines wherever man goes and lives with him for ever—is coming to us even now. This voice is like the little rivulets that come from the mountains. Now they disappear, and now they appear again in stronger flow till finally they unite in one mighty majestic flood. The messages that are coming down to us from the prophets and holy men and women of

[64] A speech by Swami Vivekananda

all sects and nations are joining their forces and speaking to us with the trumpet voice of the past. And the first message it brings us is: Peace be unto you and to all religions. It is not a message of antagonism, but of one united religion.

STOP BEING SO RELIGIOUS[65]

What Do sad people have in Common?

It seems They have all built a shrine

To the past

And often go there

And do a strange wail and Worship.

What is the beginning of Happiness?

It is to stop being

So religious Like That.

---

[65] This poem by Hafiz was translated by Daniel Ladinsky

www.ingramcontent.com/pod-product-compliance
Lightning Source LLC
LaVergne TN
LVHW010835120826
845149LV00016B/2387

* 9 7 9 8 9 8 8 5 9 1 0 0 9 *